About the Author

Dr Laura Basha – author, artist, certified trainer, and organizational psychologist – is the founder and creator of WhiteBird Rising, a resource and guide for the transformational lifestyle—a lifestyle of ongoing awakening.

She received her BFA from Beloit College, Beloit, WI. Growing up outside of Boston, MA, she has lived in northern California for the last forty years. In the process of raising her two children, her creative energies were expressed through living and working as a single mom, studying for the ministry, becoming a senior color artist for an international color consulting firm, and finally completing a master's program in counseling psychology followed by a PhD in both clinical and organizational psychology.

All of these elements began to synthesize in the last decade, when, after creating a successful consulting practice with leaders from global Fortune 1,000 companies, she is returning to her artistic roots as a published author, as well as an accomplished fine artist.

Her paintings and artwork are in private collections across the United States and in Australia. Her book, *The Inward Outlook*, is finding its way through readership around the world.

The essence of all of her creative work integrates her love of beauty, harmony, and spiritual understanding, visually expressed with archetypal and symbolic imagery. You can view her work on her website:
www.whitebirdrising.com

All Is Chosen

Laura Basha, PhD

All Is Chosen

Olympia Publishers
London

www.olympiapublishers.com
OLYMPIA PAPERBACK EDITION

Copyright ©Laura Basha, PhD 2024

The right of Laura Basha, PhD to be identified as author of this work has been asserted in accordance with sections 77 and 78 of the Copyright, Designs and Patents Act 1988.

All Rights Reserved

No reproduction, copy or transmission of this publication may be made without written permission. No paragraph of this publication may be reproduced, copied or transmitted save with the written permission of the publisher, or in accordance with the provisions of the Copyright Act 1956 (as amended).

Any person who commits any unauthorized act in relation to this publication may be liable to criminal prosecution and civil claims for damage.

A CIP catalogue record for this title is available from the British Library.

ISBN: 978-1-80439-654-4

This is a work of fiction.
Names, characters, places and incidents originate from the writer's imagination. Any resemblance to actual persons, living or dead, is purely coincidental.

First Published in 2024

Olympia Publishers
Tallis House
2 Tallis Street
London
EC4Y 0AB

Printed in Great Britain

Dedication

To those Great Beings who have gone before,
Eternally radiating the Light so that we may take the necessary next steps,
And for whom words fall short of expressing,
Deepest love and gratitude.

Acknowledgements

This handmade book is the distilled creative expression of a life-long metaphysical study, verified by years of experiences, joys and sorrows, inner battles, as well as outer accomplishments. Throughout this study, I have also had many comrades in many guises, to all whom I am deeply grateful. I name but a few below.

To my dear friend, Joan Hause, for pointing the way to these Truths. To Dru Simms, without whose guidance stemming from decades ago, my grounding in this work would not have emerged so fluidly. To Chelsea Quinn Yarbro, whose illumined first writings continue to inspire and awaken the realization and inculcation of Universal Truths. For her unwavering focus on the goal and her great spirit, many thanks to Victoria Marina-Tompkins, whose supportive work was instrumental in the creation of this book. To Larry Robinson, that rare combination of master painter with master art professor, within whose San Francisco studio most of these paintings were birthed, much gratitude for his inspirational friendship and creatively expansive guidance. To both Camden Richards and Mary Ann Casler, whose enlightened, uplifting partnership and aesthetic vision brought this inspired book to its final completion. And to my husband, Nick, for his enduring love, support, and authentic respect for my walk with these Truths. And finally, to you, the reader, my heartfelt love and appreciation. For without you, so that we walk together, the illumined flame of our birthright might lie in dormant embers.

Table of Contents

Introduction	13
On Choice	23
On Love	37
On Fear	44
Distinctions	50
The Particular Positive and Negative Polarities of the Seven Roles in Essence with The Archetypal Images	60
Conclusion	90

Introduction

How does our humanity limit us,
and how do we get free from habitual ways of thinking and acting?
How do we self-realize and quietly access our eternal essence?

What is meant by "all is chosen"? What is meant by "choice"?
How do we awaken to conscious choice?

It is my hope that the symbolic signposts to those answers lie within the poetry and paintings in this book.

Consider what arises in you as you reflect on the haikus, the colors, the textures, and the archetype images.
Consider what calls to you, what resonates to you from a deeper place as you become clear about which images draw you in.

Practice listening deeply to your own intuitive responses.
Trust them.
The archetypes and their haikus are not the message — they only point to it.
Allow them to carry you in a direction that unfolds you to yourself.

Each one of us is a combination of influences of many characteristics and traits.
Each of us is not simply one of these archetypal roles, but a combination of four,
and those four remain the heart of our true essence expression
throughout all of our many incarnations.

From the ballast of our four constant archetypes,
experienced through the multiple evolutionary cycles of reincarnation,
we come to understand every aspect of what it means to be a human being.

Rendering the archetypes in simple yet symbolic form offers a nonverbal depth of their meaning, unfolding a possible emotional response deeper than an intellectual understanding. Such depth can catalyze you into who you authentically are as their expression.

From this depth emerges knowing one's self in both positive and negative aspects.
This allows for compassionate understanding of not only the self, but of others.

Compassionate understanding brings the possibility of greater acceptance of differences, and the appreciation and celebration of those differences.

Allowing yourself to absorb the insight available through your resonance to the non-verbal communication of the archetypes, lets you perceive your eternal essence: that which cannot be affected by the never-ending changes of the physical plane.

Observing others and accepting how they might uniquely relate to the archetypes and haikus, deters the impulse to try and change their perspective.

Thinking gets in the way of seeing Oneness.

Let us awaken to the common thread of Love that runs through all of us as we evolve away from attachment to the many faces of maya with its seductive grip of fear.

Let us practice being present, in the moment of now — no attention paid to thinking.
Over-identification with thinking results in suffering.

Underneath our individual uniqueness is the Truth of Oneness.

We have an identity in form: our bodies and personalities.

We have Essence identity
—our true Self—
which is the expression of eternal Source through us.

Freedom from suffering arises when we know ourselves as this immortal essence.

May these archetypal images of the Roles in Essence awaken in you the remembrance of who you truly are.

On Choice

All is chosen.

Choice will occur, either through love or fear.
This is a Universal Truth.

To agree or not with these statements is also a choice.
Yet, when examined, the validity of the statements emerge.

Without the awareness of the ability to choose, and without awareness of the freedom to make any choice in any situation, there is the belief that something or someone outside of the individual is dictating what will be chosen.

Certainly there are circumstances outside of our control or influence, yet there is always the choice of how to be with any circumstance, or what meaning to make of any given moment.

That choice will occur is a Universal Truth. However, why a choice is made is a personal truth.

It is powerful to remember that our personal choices determine the quality of our life experience.

All choice is valid, and all choice leads eventually to growth and development.

However, it really is in our purview to create a life experience where we choose to be responsible for making choices from our most positive and insightful thinking.

This kind of responsibility of consciously choosing which thoughts to act upon gives us a grace in living, and an unflappable sense of stability.
There is then more access to the capacity for being present in the moment.

Are we unconsciously choosing, thus a victim to our own thinking, or are we consciously choosing, thus aware of our thinking, being the conscious creator of our own experience?

True action takes place first in thought.
Awakening to such conscious mastery is available to all.

By allowing ourselves to begin to become aware that choice remains a viable truth at all times, it is more likely that a sense of personal mastery will emerge.

"I choose" could be a good mantra to bring our attention to the truth of choice.

Practicing in everyday matters
—such as, which shoes do I choose to wear today?—
can begin to develop expertise in the process of choosing consciously in other areas of life.

Choices made from fear have certain characteristics. Recognizing these characteristics can assist you in identifying the source of the choice.

Choices made from fear can include indecision, confusion, and/or apprehension.
There can be arrogance, judgement and intolerance, abuse of power, haste, intensity, or control.

Sometimes we are duped as these fear-based choices can masquerade as good sense, or best for all concerned, when in fact they are fueled by survival of the identity, the false personality.

Choices made from fear feel seductively inclusive, undermining the authentic expression of essence.

Choices made from love have the sense of simplicity, neither looking for approval nor having any conditions attached.

Choices made from love are usually clear and inconspicuous, being made from Essence.

Choices made from love feel like fresh air.

It is from the character of the response to a situation which will determine if the next choice will be from love or fear, or even indifference, which is another form of fear.

One way to begin to distinguish whether a choice is made from love or fear is to consider if the choice is being made without conditions.

Willingness to embrace the concept of choice and inquire into patterns of personal response can illumine which choices are made from fear, and which choices are made from love.

Unconscious choosing can be elevated to conscious choosing when we take action in the outer while listening from the inner.

Recognizing this process is a powerful first step in making choices from love rather than fear, and thus can assist a person in validating the source of their choice.

Fear contracts. Love expands.

Fear creates distance. Love embraces, for there is no separation.

Fear regards with righteousness, contempt and judgement. Love regards with compassion.

Fear choices create a life experience of judgement and distance, while choices made from love create a life experience of compassion and expansion.

There is always a choice point of how and from which perspective to take action.

Life is a rehearsal for life.

On Love

It is Love that prevails throughout the universe as the highest guiding Light.

Love is the path of Essence, the path of Oneness.

Love is Home.

Love is the highest Truth.

It is through Love, the expression of Essence, that one can rise above the constraints and confines of the personality in order to be available for essence contact.

Essence contact is the point of evolution.

When we are able to foster love in the life, from love of self, to love of children, to love of nature, then we are much better able to be open to making direct contact, essence contact, with our fellows.

It is through such moments as these that real and true evolutionary progress is made.

Love does not have requirements.
Love only loves.

Love does not demand.
Love is acceptance and in its highest form, Agape, which is the true nature of compassion.

Love without conditions breaks down the barriers of fear and opens the way to communion and Joy.

Love has no needs; it simply is.

Love is the creative dynamic force that resonates throughout the Universe and sees no distinction between all that exists.

Love sees only Love.

On Fear

It is well known that fear is strong.

Only Love is stronger than fear.

This is a Universal Truth.

When fear is strong, the creative resources within a person become less available, and sometimes completely inaccessible.

This leads to the belief that there are no other choices possible except the ones that have already been offered, which are usually the socially acceptable ones.

Many of us will choose to follow the socially acceptable choices and ignore the voice of essence, which is subsequently buried in the depths of unconsciousness in order to avoid the disruptive challenge of authentic expression.

Fear does assist in processing the lessons of what it means to be in our human bodies.

Fear can exacerbate these lessons, as well as assist in survival situations, such as when one's life is threatened.

It takes some investigation to become consciously aware that fear is a *choice*, albeit sometimes a "sensible" one in certain circumstances.

It is possible, however, to relinquish fear, to relinquish control and find one's peace, even if death is the possible outcome.

It is possible to process the lessons of the physical plane through Joy.

Let us remember that Essence, that part of us which is immortal and eternal, remains unaffected by fear.

It is the return to Love that offers the path to liberation.

Distinctions

The Positive and Negative Polarities of the Archetypal Roles in Essence

Each Role in Essence has a positive and negative polarity, or outlook.

Each positive or negative outlook has a particular expression that is informed either by love or by fear.

Whatever our roles in essence, each of us has available both the positive and negative expressions of the characteristics of our chosen roles.

It behooves us to become consciously aware of our positive outlooks as well as, and perhaps even more importantly, of our own particular negative outlooks.

Awareness of the negative points the way out into the positive expression.

The negative polarities of each individual archetypal role are the expression of fear, with particular identifiable fear characteristics.

These fears are a part of experiencing life on the physical plane.

Still, taking actions from them is a choice.

Once aware of your negative characteristics, it is as if a light shone on the main issue to be addressed.

Such awareness allows you to be authentically and powerfully creative, inspired in the action of choosing.

The negative expression is essentially the block to authenticity — the block to the expression of love.

With awareness, you can then re-think choice, able to contribute through choosing from the positive polarity of love.

Love chooses fulfilling and meaningful ways to express, benefitting not only you, but also all those in your world.

Without judgement, we give ourselves the gift of awareness of *both* sides of the polarities, so that we can *consciously choose* how to express ourselves in any given situation.

It is possible for a person to change a viewpoint from the negative to the positive, which allows for the positive polarity of a role to emerge.

We can choose not to engage with fear.

That inner battle is fierce and full of challenges when efforts are made to silence and dissolve those fears.

However, the willingness to consciously engage in such a challenge is the path to true inner freedom and peace of mind, and opens the door for a more rich life experience.

As each of us awakens to our own archetypal roles, our own connection to essence, our individual awakening catalyzes awakening in all who think of us, all who speak of us, and in all whom we contact.

An expanded awakening in human consciousness emerges.

The Particular Positive and Negative Polarities of the Seven Roles in Essence
with
The Archetypal Images
including
"Zero": Rest and Reflection Between Lives for Evaluative and Design Purposes

Each Role in Essence has particular characteristics of fear that are called upon every day by each of us, according to the particular choice of fear made.

The fears are seven, to match each Role:
The fear of inadequacy
The fear of loss of control
The fear of lacking value or worthiness
The fear of change
The fear of lack or want
The fear of missing out
and
The fear of vulnerability.

They each have their own characteristics or flavor, and are each a particular cornerstone of our created personality.

It is important to note that one can choose, and often does, two from the seven fears, two fear expressions that may or may not match those fears "naturally" belonging to the four chosen Roles in Essence.

In other words, you could be a Role in Essence of ONE with a chosen primary fear that "naturally" matches FOUR.

Or you could be a Role in Essence of THREE, choosing a primary fear that "naturally" matches SIX.

I

Key Fear: Fear of inadequacy (Self-Deprecation)

When positive and love-based, the polarity expression of ONE expresses as service through a dedication to the well-being of others, and in particular, care for the young and care for the elderly.

When negative, the polarity expression of ONE is through fear, when the dedication is tethered to another person or group of persons, and the service is bound to the other without regard for the self.

I

The child at her feet
All things prepared for the day
Harvest from the earth

II

Key Fear: Fear of loss of control (Self-Destruction)

When positive and love-based, the polarity expression of TWO is creation, where the unique is created through a painting, a music composition, or a new recipe. The positive polarity may be seen as authentic.

When negative and fear-based, the polarity expression of TWO is artifice, which simply copies what it sees, and is not new or unique. The negative pole may be seen as artificial, or inauthentic.

II

Colors swirl by design
Awake the creative muse!
Formless to form.

III

Key Fear: Fear of lack of value or worthiness (Martyrdom)

When positive and love-based, the polarity expression of THREE is persuasion, where THREE is able to bring others around to their point of view without fear, e.g., "you can make this choice and here is why…". The positive expression of THREE opens the door to alignment.

When negative and fear-based, the polarity expression of THREE attempts to wrangle the other person into acting or believing in a certain way. The negative expression of THREE attempts to push through the door, through intimidation or manipulation.

III

Strong of heart and will
Pledged allegiance to the cause
Loyal friend, steel-eyed foe.

IV

Key Fear: Fear of change (Stubbornness)

When positive and love-based, the polarity expression of FOUR is knowledge, where FOUR will apply his or her understanding and database to his or her life. The natural and positive attitude of FOUR is to be the pragmatist and thereby apply knowledge in such a way as to create a workable and sensible life.

When negative and fear-based, the polarity expression of FOUR is theory, where FOUR stays in theory without practical application. Coming from theory, there is much head spinning and head scratching without practical usage.

IV

Knowledge, words expound
Scholarly tomes of incarnations lived
Introspective, quietude.

V

Key Fear: Fear of lack or want (Greed)

When positive and love-based, the positive polarity expression of FIVE is authentic expression, where FIVE will take the audience response into account. The positive expression of FIVE is through the communication of truths as perceived by FIVE with careful attention to verbiage usage.

When negative and fear-based, the polarity expression of FIVE is oration, or talking without meaning or substance. Communication becomes only a performance that does not take the audience response into account.

V

Set the stage for play!
Merriment abounds, words cast
To all who will hear.

VI

Key Fear: Fear of vulnerability (Arrogance)

When positive and love-based, the positive polarity expression of SIX is compassion. SIX offers solace to others through a compassionate understanding of the issues at hand.

When negative and fear-based, the polarity expression of SIX is zeal. In this negative stance SIX maintains truth as he or she perceives it to be, i.e., the "only way to God or enlightenment".

VI

Lux Aeterna, Shines
Radiant beauty uplifts
Remembering God.

VII

Key Fear: Fear of missing out (Impatience)

When positive and love-based, the positive polarity of SEVEN is mastery. SEVEN leads in a masterful and regal way with knowledge of the needs of his or her "kingdom".

When negative and fear-based, the negative polarity of SEVEN is tyranny. Here in the negative polarity expression, SEVEN rules through fear, which includes maintaining an iron fist with punitive results.

Coronation begins,
Pageantry heralds the King
Chosen to rule the land.

Zero

Different from the other seven archetypal images, ZERO is the common archetype experienced by all souls between lives. It is not part of the physical plane archetypal choices, although it can be accessed energetically.

It is included in the text and images of this book, as it is an archetype experienced by all once the particular end-of-life physical transition is made.

When positive and love-based, the polarity expression of ZERO is expressed as ingenuity or imagination. The positive polarity sees the many possibilities when creating the life plan, including all choices related to creating the next life experience.

When negative and fear-based, the polarity expression of ZERO is simply embarkation. There is participation in the ensoulment process yet it is without enthusiasm.

Adventure beckons!
A moment out of time
Imminent birth of the Soul.

Conclusion

Life experience is interesting, wouldn't you say?

I am a professional artist and published author.
I have birthed and raised two children and experienced with them the early tragic death of their father.
I was a single working mother while going through graduate school, and I also studied for the ministry.
I am stepmother to three, "Nona" to nine, and essentially have experienced like you, so many of the ups and downs of living life on the physical plane.

As a psychologist, therapist and coach, I have powerfully and successfully worked with young children, families, couples, teenagers, teachers, administrative personnel, dentists, physicians, business executives, business leaders, artists, psychiatrists, psychologists, therapists, the persistently mentally ill population, school systems, corporations, non-profit organizations, and the general public.

I have powerfully and successfully worked inter-culturally, spoken at conferences, appeared on public television, been interviewed on the radio, given workshops, headed up corporate restructuring trainings, and attended hundreds of hours of my own ongoing personal development.

So… why write this book on this subject?

I want to creatively share some of the underpinnings of successful transformational work with people from all walks of life. Opinions about gender, age, and cultural differences complicate what is useful in assisting people from getting free from suffering and the limitations of the past.

We are all, in truth, in the same boat.
Perceived differences are of the world of transient form.
Transient form comes and goes.
All that is living dies and returns to dust, or more accurately, to the One Substance out of which All Things are formed.

Form is temporal.
Human beings are of the world of form, the physical plane reality.
Who we are as eternal beings is just that: eternal. With understanding of the invisible eternal fabric of which we are all threads, we can be less trapped by the seduction of form.
And if we so choose, we can then access the freedom of eternality while temporarily visiting the physical plane in our human bodies.

This study, if you are willing to consider it as possibility, can free you from suffering.

It won't free you from the challenges of life experience, for we are all here to learn and evolve.
But braving to pull the veil back far enough to witness, and perhaps even inculcate, the eternal
Truths upon which we reliably rest, will allow you to navigate the challenges of the physical plane with stability, equanimity, and peace of mind.

It is possible to experience all of life from compassion and Joy rather than fear, pain, and suffering. We are not very practiced at that. How extraordinary would it be to catalyze the awakening of Joy within ourselves, and thus to our fellows?
What would experience on our planet be like if we could deal with the vicissitudes of life with the compassion and confidence born of Joy?

So again… why create this book?

Choice, Love, Fear, the seven archetypal Roles in Essence, as well as the archetypal interval Role between lives, are but a few of the Universal Truths which resonate throughout all physical plane realms.

Universal Truths interpenetrate the consciousness of all forms of sentient beings.
This means Universal Truth is available to all of us, according to our level of awareness.

Inculcating this perception allows us to awaken to the realization of Oneness.
We can awaken not to an unfounded ideology, but to a ballast which can free us from bondage to the illusion of separateness.

Each Role in Essence has a perceptual difference in how it approaches life experience.
Understanding these perceptual differences allows for a curious listening of others, rather than judging others or trying to persuade or coerce them to your point of view.

Seeing life from a different perceptual vantage point can simply become fascinating, as opposed to challenging or threatening. Becoming familiar with the differing perceptions intrinsic to each Role in Essence brings a grounded ease in living. We can begin to see that different perspectives do not impinge on freedom. Rather acceptance of different perspectives brings ease and freedom to relationships, as well as to the life of self and others.

This acceptance facilitates a return to seeing the Oneness of all sentient beings. Differences in form distract us into thinking there is an inherent difference between us.
Yet it is the One formless energetic frequency within each differing form of each Role, through various expressions over many lifetimes, that awakens the realization of Oneness.

The realization of this Oneness foreshadows the realization of the eventual return to the Tao, the Source of All That Is.

Awakening to Oneness expands the capacity to be present, in the moment, accepting what is in form with the wisdom of knowing its temporality.
We are accustomed to learning through pain and struggle.
We are not particularly practiced in learning through Joy.
Yet it is possible to learn through Joy.

Life experience is meant to be challenging.
Freedom from struggle in the face of challenge is available through awakening to these Universal Truths.